TALK LIKE AN AUSSIE
THE AUSTRALIAN SLANG PHRASEBOOK FOR TRAVELERS

Welcome to Talk Like an Aussie, your ultimate guide to mastering Australian slang and connecting with locals during your travels! This book is designed specifically for travelers who want to go beyond basic English and dive into the colorful, quirky, and sometimes hilarious world of Aussie speech.

Inside, you'll find just the essential terms that will help you navigate everyday conversations, from greetings like "G'day mate" to food-related phrases like "sanga" (sandwich). Each term comes with:
- A simple definition to make learning easy.
- Real-life examples of use so you can see how Aussies incorporate these words into their daily language.
- The origin or background of the term gives you deeper insight into Australian culture.
- Practical tips for using the phrase naturally in conversation.

Whether you're ordering a "flat white" at a café, chatting about the weather ("pissing down sideways"), or teasing a friend about being a "dag," this book has everything you need to sound like a true-blue Aussie. With categorized chapters, an A-Z glossary, and a bonus section on humorous idioms, Talk Like an Aussie ensures you're prepared for any situation from casual barbecues to outdoor adventures.

Get ready to enhance your travel experience, impress locals, and enjoy the laugh-out-loud moments of speaking Australia's unique lingo!

Contents

Navigate Your Book by Categories

Chapter 1: Greetings & Politeness ———————————— 5

Chapter 2: Food & Drinks ———————————— 17

Chapter 3: Nature & Outdoors ———————————— 27

Chapter 4: Socializing & Culture ———————————— 42

Chapter 5: Travel & Transport ———————————— 53

Chapter 6: Quirky & Funny Words ———————————— 69

Chapter 7: Witty Wisdom: Aussie Idioms and Playful Phrases ———————— 77

Navigate by A to Z: Comprehensive Slang Glossary

A —	87	N —	91
B —	87	O —	91
C —	88	P —	92
D —	88	Q —	...
E —	89	R —	92
F —	89	S —	92
G —	89	T —	93
H —	90	U —	94
I —	...	V —	...
J —	90	W —	94
K —	90	X —	...
L —	91	Y —	94
M —	91	Z —	94

Chapter 1:
Greetings & Politeness

Welcome to Australia, where greetings extend beyond just "Hello" and "Thank you." In this section, you'll explore typical Australian expressions for saying "Hi" inquiring about someone's well-being, and expressing appreciation. From the informal "Mate" to the traditional "No worries," mastering these phrases will help you blend in like a local. Discover how to confidently greet Australians, respond courteously, and foster connections during your journey. You'll be amazed at how much a simple "Ta" or "Cheers" can achieve!

Bonza

- Meaning: A flexible word that signifies something outstanding, superb, or wonderful. Ideal for conveying excitement or offering a courteous compliment.
- Cultural Context: Thought to have come from the Aboriginal term "banza," which translates to good or authentic. It has evolved into a cherished element of Australian slang over the years.
- Example Usage: "The food at the restaurant was bonza!" or "You did a bonza job organizing the trip."

- Tips for Use: This term is well-known and valued for its favorable meaning. Feel free to use it when complimenting something or someone; it will bring joy!

Bloody Oath!

- Meaning: A powerful way to agree, akin to saying "Definitely!" or "For sure!"
- Cultural Context: This phrase merges "bloody," an intensifying word frequently found in Australian English, with "oath," highlighting assurance. It showcases the direct and enthusiastic style of communication typical in Australia.
- Example Usage: "Are you coming to the barbecue tonight?" "Bloody oath, I wouldn't miss it!"
- Tips for Use: Although "bloody" is frequently used in informal discussions, it may be viewed as rude in formal situations. Therefore, using it cautiously when interacting with new acquaintances or in professional environments is advisable.

Bring a Plate

- Meaning: A courteous invitation for attendees to bring food to share at an event, like a party or family gathering.
- Cultural Context: This phrase is based on the communal nature of Australian culture, promoting collective contribution and enjoyment.
- Example Usage: "We're having a potluck dinner this weekend; just bring a plate!"
- Tips for Use: Bringing a dish to a social gathering not only eases the host's responsibilities but also demonstrates consideration. Common options include desserts, salads, or savory treats.

Catch Ya Later

- Meaning: An informal way to say farewell, similar to "See you later."
- Cultural Context: As with many expressions in Australia, it's a condensed and casual form of a longer phrase, showcasing the relaxed nature of Australians.
- Example Usage: "I've gotta head out now; catch ya later!"
- Tips for Use: This phrase is suitable for informal goodbyes. It's warm and casual, making it ideal for regular conversations.

Cheers

- Meaning: A flexible word used to show appreciation, say goodbye, or wish someone well.
- Cultural Context: "Cheers" started as a British expression and has been adopted by Australians, finding its way into various situations, from expressing thanks to celebrating.
- Example Usage:
    - Thanks: "Cheers for helping me move the furniture."
    - Goodbye: "Catch ya tomorrow, cheers!"
    - Toasting: "Let's raise a glass. Cheers to good times ahead!"

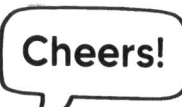

- Tips for Use: The adaptability of "cheers" makes it one of the most practical terms in Australian English. It's suitable for expressing gratitude or concluding a conversation.

Excuse Me/Sorry

- Meaning: These are courteous phrases used to express apologies or to interrupt someone.
- Cultural Context: Widely used in English-speaking cultures, these expressions are crucial for maintaining polite communication in Australia.
- Example Usage:
    - Apology: "Oops, sorry about that!"
    - Interruption: "Excuse me, could you tell me where the nearest café is?"
- Tips for Use: In Australia, being polite is very important. Appropriately using "excuse me" or "sorry" can help you integrate smoothly with the local community.

Fair Go

- Definition/Explanation: A plea for equity or opportunity, representing the egalitarian principles of Australian culture.
- Origin/History: Firmly rooted in Australian society, "fair go" signifies the conviction that everyone is entitled to an opportunity, irrespective of their background.
- Example Usage:
    - Request: "Give him a fair go. He's new to the team."
    - Assertion: "All I'm asking for is a fair go!"
- Additional Notes: This expression is emblematic in Australia and frequently appears in conversations about equality and justice. Adopting "fair go" demonstrates an appreciation for local values and customs.

Good on Ya

- Meaning: A cheerful expression used to convey "well done" or "good job." It serves as a warm and encouraging remark.
- Cultural Context: This phrase embodies the supportive and community-focused spirit of Australian culture. It is frequently employed to commend someone for their hard work or accomplishments.
- Example Usage: "You aced that exam. Good on ya!"
- Tips for Use: Utilize this expression to express gratitude or admiration. It is ideal for informal situations and enhances the genuineness of your discussions.

G'day

- Meaning: A traditional Australian greeting that translates to "hello" or "good day."
- Cultural Context: This phrase is a contraction of "good day" and gained popularity in the early 1900s, becoming a symbol of Australian friendliness.
- Example Usage: "G'day mate," "How ya goin'?"

- Tips for Use: Using "G'day" alongside "mate" is a quintessential Australian expression. It's an excellent way to initiate a conversation and quickly bond with locals.

Hooroo

- Meaning: A somewhat outdated yet still popular expression for "goodbye."
- Cultural Context: Originating from "Hooray," it serves as a cheerful and casual send-off that embodies the easygoing nature of Australians.
- Example Usage: "I need to leave now. Hooroo!"
- Tips for Use: Although it isn't as frequently used as other ways to say goodbye, "hooroo" carries a sense of nostalgia. Using it could bring a smile to the faces of older Australians!

How Ya Goin'?

- Meaning: A relaxed way of inquiring about someone's well-being or current situation.
- Cultural Context: This expression reflects the straightforward and informal nature of communication in Australia.
- Example Usage: "Hey, how ya goin', mate? Haven't seen you in ages!"
- Tips for Use: It's common for Australians to jump right into this question after a brief greeting, as it helps establish a quick connection.

How's It Garn?

- Meaning: A different way of saying "How's it going?" is commonly used in rural or regional settings.
- Cultural Context: Probably originating from Cockney slang, this expression has become a part of the Australian language and is still frequently used.
- Example Usage: "How's it garn, mate? Had a good weekend?"
- Tips for Use: While this phrase may seem unusual to those unfamiliar with it, it is well-recognized and brings a unique flair to casual conversations.

How's the Form?

- Meaning: A lighthearted way to inquire about someone's well-being or how things are going in their life.
- Cultural Context: This expression comes from horse racing, where "form" indicates a horse's performance history, and it amusingly extends that idea to individuals.
- Example Usage: "Not seen you in ages, how's the form?"
- Tips for Use: This phrase can make your greetings more enjoyable and is particularly useful when reconnecting with friends or acquaintances.

How's the Serenity?

- Meaning: A playful variation of "how's it going?" that literally means "how's the peace?"
- Cultural Context: This expression emphasizes the pursuit of calmness or tranquility in everyday life, showcasing Australia's fondness for humor and clever language.
- Example Usage: "Hey mate, how's the serenity? Still keeping busy?"
- Tips for Use: Ideal for starting a conversation or adding a touch of humor. Australians enjoy witty expressions like this.

How's Tricks?

- Definition/Explanation: A relaxed way of inquiring about someone's well-being or recent happenings.

- Cultural Context: Probably derived from British slang, this expression has become common in Australian conversation because of its straightforward and friendly nature.
- Example Usage: "Long time no see, how's tricks?"
- Tips for Use: This phrase is suitable for both formal and casual situations, making it adaptable for various interactions.

Mate

- Meaning: A term used to address friends, acquaintances, or even strangers in a friendly manner.
- Cultural Context: Deeply embedded in Australian culture, "mate" reflects the importance of camaraderie and friendship.
- Example Usage: "G'day mate, how ya goin'?" or "Cheers, mate, for the help."
- Tips for Use: Whether you're chatting with a close friend or striking up a conversation with a stranger, "mate" is a universally accepted term of endearment.

No worries

- Meaning: A courteous way to respond with "you're welcome" or "it's all good." It can also serve to comfort others that things will be okay.
- Cultural Context: This expression reflects the laid-back nature of Australians, who favor a relaxed approach to life.
- Example Usage: "Thanks for picking me up!" "No worries, happy to help."

- Tips for Use: Feel free to use "No worries" frequently. It's a classic Australian phrase that will help you blend in like a local quickly.

Not Bad, Thanks

- Meaning: A courteous reply to the question "How are you?" suggesting that everything is fine without elaborating.
- Cultural Context: This expression reflects a blend of politeness and restraint, in line with the Australian tendency towards modesty.
- Example Usage: "How are you?" "Not bad, thanks. what about you?"
- Tips for Use: If you're uncertain about what to say, "Not bad, thanks" is a reliable option. It maintains a light and friendly tone in conversation.

Oath!

- Meaning: A strong expression of agreement, similar to "absolutely!" or "hell yes!"
- Cultural Context: Likely shortened from "bloody oath," this phrase emphasizes sincerity and enthusiasm.
- Example Usage: "Are you going to the footy match?" "Oath, I wouldn't skip it for anything!"
- Tips for Use: While "oath" alone is less intense than "bloody oath," it still conveys excitement and agreement. Use it when you want to show enthusiasm without swearing.

Pardon?/Eh?

- Meaning: A courteous or informal method of requesting someone to repeat their statement.
- Cultural Context: These expressions highlight the significance of effective communication in Australian culture, facilitating straightforward clarification without causing discomfort.
- Example Usage: "What time is the meeting again? Pardon?" or "Eh, did you say tomorrow or today?"
- Tips for Use: Both "Pardon?" and "Eh" are commonly used based on the degree of formality. Use "Pardon?" in more formal situations and "Eh" in casual discussions.

Reckon

- Meaning: An informal expression meaning "I think" or "I believe," commonly used in friendly conversations.
- Cultural Context: Originating from British English, "reckon" has become a common part of Australian vernacular because of its casual nature.
- Example Usage: "Reckon it'll rain later?" or "I reckon we should head out soon."
- Tips for Use: This phrase is ideal for sharing thoughts or proposing ideas in a way that feels less forceful.

Righto

- Meaning: A casual and friendly way to agree, similar to saying "okay" or "all right."
- Cultural Context: This term is a contraction of "right oh," showcasing the direct and uncomplicated style of communication typical in Australia.
- Example Usage: "Shall we meet at 6 PM?" "Righto, see you then!"
- Tips for Use: Use "righto" to confirm plans or details. It conveys a relaxed yet effective tone.

Seeya

- Meaning: A casual expression for saying "goodbye."
- Cultural Context: This term is a contraction of "see you" and is a typical instance of Australian slang.
- Example Usage: "I've gotta run now. Seeya later!"
- Tips for Use: Similar to other Australian goodbyes, "Seeya" has a cheerful and informal tone, making it perfect for relaxed farewells.

She'll Be Right

- Meaning: A reassuring phrase meaning "it's okay" or "everything will work out fine."
- Cultural Context: This iconic phrase embodies the laid-back, optimistic attitude of Australians, encouraging calmness in challenging situations.
- Example Usage: "The car broke down. what do we do?" "She'll be right, let's call a mechanic."

- Tips for Use: Use this phrase to comfort others or reassure yourself when things go wrong. It's a quintessential piece of Aussie wisdom.

Stone the Crows!

- Meaning: An expression used to convey shock, disbelief, or surprise.
- Cultural Context: The precise origin is uncertain, but it probably comes from earlier slang phrases that included animals. Today, it serves as a lighthearted way to express amazement.
- Example Usage: "Stone the crows, did you really win the lottery?"
- Tips for Use: Although this phrase is less frequently used by younger people, it brings a unique flair to your conversation and reflects a fondness for classic Australian humor.

Struth!

- Meaning: A gentle expression of astonishment or skepticism, akin to "Is that really the case?" or "Incredible!"
- Cultural Context: Derived from "God's truth," this expression has transformed into a playful response to surprising information.
- Example Usage: "Struth, I can't believe you scaled that mountain!"
- Tips for Use: Incorporate "goodness" to infuse a bit of vintage flair into your responses. It works particularly well in storytelling or reminiscing.

Ta Ra

- Meaning: A casual expression for "goodbye."
- Cultural Context: Probably originating from "ta ta," this phrase reflects the Australian tendency for brevity and friendliness.

- Example Usage: "I appreciate your visit, ta ra for now!"
- Tips for Use: Combine "ta ra" with a smile or wave for a friendly farewell. It's concise, pleasant, and easy to remember.

Ta

- Meaning: An informal expression of gratitude, equivalent to "thank you."
- Cultural Context: This term comes from British slang and has become commonly used in Australia because of its friendly and straightforward nature.
- Example Usage: "Here's your coffee." "Ta, mate!"

- Tips for Use: "Ta" is a great way to convey thanks quickly and casually. It's one of the most adaptable ways to say thank you.

Too Easy

- Meaning: A casual expression meaning "no problem" or "that's straightforward."
- Cultural Context: This phrase embodies the laid-back attitude of Australians, assuring others that requests or tasks are not a hassle.
- Example Usage: "Could you help me lift this box?" "Too easy, not a problem!"
- Tips for Use: Ideal for indicating readiness to help or downplaying worries about the effort involved. It's a signature of Australian friendliness.

Tuckeroo

- Meaning: A casual expression for saying "goodbye."
- Cultural Context: While not as widely used as other forms of farewell, "tuckeroo" has a playful and unique feel, reminiscent of older Australian slang.
- Example Usage: "See you later, tuckeroo!"
- Tips for Use: This phrase should be used occasionally to bring a touch of nostalgia or humor to your goodbyes, making it memorable in discussions.

You Right?

- Meaning: A relaxed way to inquire if someone is alright or requires assistance.
- Cultural Context: This expression merges concern with practicality, showcasing the helpful spirit of Australian communication.
- Example Usage: "You seem a little confused, are you right?" or "Do you require directions?"
- Tips for Use: Employ "you right?" to check on someone or subtly provide help. It conveys both care and respect.

Chapter 2:
Food & Drinks

Australia's food culture is as vibrant as its unique slang! This section explores terms such as "Sanga" (Sandwich) and "Coldie" (Beer). By learning food-related slang, you'll enhance your dining experiences, whether you're ordering at cafes or enjoying meals with locals. Discover why "Parma" is a favorite, what makes "Tucker" special, and how to impress your friends with your knowledge of "Flat whites." Get ready to converse like a true Aussie when it comes to food and drinks!

Anzac Biscuit

- Meaning: A traditional Australian cookie made with oats, golden syrup, coconut, and flour, named in honor of the ANZAC (Australian and New Zealand Army Corps) soldiers from World War I.
- Cultural Context: Created as a durable snack for soldiers, Anzac biscuits have evolved into a symbol of remembrance and are particularly popular on ANZAC Day (April 25).
- Example Usage: "I baked some Anzac biscuits for morning tea, would you like one?"
- Tips for Use: These biscuits are cherished for their chewy consistency and sweet taste, making them ideal for sharing with friends or enjoying a cup of tea.

Barbie

- Meaning: A colloquial term for "barbecue," it pertains to both the process of grilling food and the tools utilized for it.
- Cultural Context: Barbecues are an integral part of Australian culture, frequently linked to outdoor events and festivities.
- Example Usage: "Let's fire up the Barbie for lunch!"

- Tips for Use: Australians enjoy hosting barbecues, particularly in the summer. Typical foods served include sausages (snags), chops, and seafood.

Bikkie

- Meaning: A colloquial term for a biscuit or cookie.
- Cultural Context: Reflecting Australia's tendency to shorten words, "bikkie" is derived from "biscuit."
- Example Usage: "Would you like a bikkie with your tea?"
- Tips for Use: This term is commonly used in daily conversations, whether referring to a chocolate chip bikkie or a plain one.

Brekky

- Meaning: An informal and abbreviated term for "breakfast."
- Cultural Context: Australians tend to shorten everyday words, and "brekky" is a prime example.
- Example Usage: "What do we have for brekky today?"

- Tips for Use: The term "brekky" is suitable for discussing morning meals in a casual and friendly manner.

Bubble and Squeak

- Meaning: A classic dish created by frying leftover vegetables, usually potatoes and cabbage, until they become crispy.
- Cultural Context: The name is derived from the bubbling and squeaking noises the vegetables produce during cooking. It's an economical and tasty method for utilizing leftovers.
- Example Usage: "I've got some bubble and squeak for dinner, hope you're hungry!"
- Tips for Use: Although it may not be as popular as other meals, bubble and squeak continue to be cherished by those who appreciate hearty, homemade cuisine.

Chook

- Meaning: A colloquial term for chicken, applicable to both the animal and its meat.
- Cultural Context: The word "chook" comes from Old English and has been a staple in Australian slang for many years.
- Example Usage: "We're having roast chook for dinner tonight."
- Tips for Use: This term is commonly used in informal discussions related to food or agriculture.

Coldie

- Meaning: A casual term referring to a cold beer.
- Cultural Context: Australians enjoy a chilled drink, and "coldie" emerged as a convenient way to refer to their preferred beverage.

Friend 1: "Who fancies a coldie before we head home?"

Friend 2: "Nah, I'm good just grab me a cold soda instead. But make sure it's as refreshing as your coldie !"

- Tips for Use: Whether it's a stubby (small bottle) or a tinny (can), a coldic is always appreciated after a tiring day.

Cuppa

- Meaning: A relaxed way to refer to a cup of tea or coffee.
- Cultural Context: Similar to various Australian expressions, "cuppa" is a shortened version of "cup of tea."
- Example Usage: "Let's sit down with a cuppa and chat about your plans for the trip"

- Tips for Use: Inviting someone for a cuppa is a courteous act and is a key aspect of everyday life in Australia.

Dead Horse

- Meaning: A colloquial term for tomato sauce or ketchup.
- Cultural Context: The exact origin of this phrase is uncertain, but it may have originated from old jokes about how to improve the taste of "dead horse."
- Example Usage: "Pass the dead horse, would you? I want some on my chips."
- Tips for Use: Australians have a strong fondness for dead horse (ketchup), making it a common condiment for a variety of foods, including sausages and fries.

Dim Sim

- Meaning: A deep-fried dumpling influenced by Chinese cuisine, typically filled with pork or beef and vegetables.
- Cultural Context: Dim sims were developed in Australia in the early 20th century, blending Chinese and Australian culinary traditions.
- Example Usage: "I'm craving some dim sims for lunch, what about you?"
- Tips for Use: Dim sims are commonly found in many fish-and-chip shops, offering a distinctive take on traditional Asian dumplings.

Dog's Eye

- Meaning: A colloquial term for a meat pie, which is a savory pastry filled with minced meat and gravy.
- Cultural Context: The term probably originates from the notion that the round shape of pies resembles eyes when they are baked.
- Example Usage: "How about we pick up a dog's eye from the bakery since it's lunchtime?"

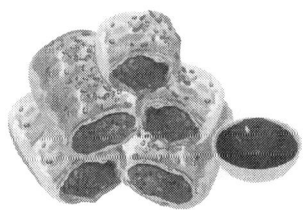

- Tips for Use: Meat pies are a quintessential Australian snack, ideal for picnics, sports events, or convenient meals on the move.

Fairy Bread

- Meaning: Slices of buttered bread topped with vibrant sprinkles, commonly found at children's celebrations.
- Cultural Context: This delightful snack has been popular with both children and adults since the early 1900s.
- Example Usage: "The kids went crazy for the fairy bread at the birthday party!"a
- Tips for Use: Fairy bread is a straightforward yet cherished treat, representing joy and festivity in Australian culture.

Flat White

- Meaning: A coffee beverage consisting of espresso and steamed milk, it is more robust than a latte yet creamier than a cappuccino.
- Cultural Context: The origins of the flat white are contested between Australia and New Zealand, but it is generally accepted as a creation from the Australasian region.
- Example Usage: "Could I get a flat white, please? I prefer it strong."
- Tips for Use: For coffee enthusiasts traveling to Australia, trying a flat white is essential, as it highlights the country's passion for quality coffee.

Lamington

- Meaning: A sponge cake that is covered in chocolate icing and rolled in coconut, named after Lord Lamington, who was a former governor of Queensland.
- Cultural Context: Lamingtons were first made in the late 1800s and continue to be a beloved treat in Australia.
- Example Usage: "Mum made lamingtons for afternoon tea, help yourself!"
- Tips for Use: These cakes are a staple of Australian baking culture and are commonly found at fundraisers and family events.

Lollies

- Meaning: Refers to candies or sweets, such as chocolates, gummies, and hard candies.
- Cultural Context: A broad term commonly used in Australia, showcasing the nation's fondness for sugary treats.
- Example Usage: "Does anyone want some lollies? I have jellybeans and chocolates!"

- Tips for Use: Lollies are a favored snack for both children and adults, often found at parties and during movie nights.

Parma

- Meaning: A shortened term for chicken parmigiana, which consists of breaded chicken covered with tomato sauce, cheese, and occasionally ham.
- Cultural Context: Brought to Australia by Italian immigrants, the parma has become a staple in pubs across the country.
- Example Usage: "For dinner, I think I'll order a parma, it's always a safe choice."
- Tips for Use: Numerous pubs have their unique versions of the parma, contributing to its status as one of the most popular dishes in Australia.

Pavlova

- Meaning: A dessert made from meringue, usually garnished with whipped cream and fresh fruit.
- Cultural Context: Both Australia and New Zealand assert that they invented pavlova, which is a popular treat during the holiday season.
- Example Usage: "Let's finish the meal with a slice of pavlova. It's light and refreshing!"

- Tips for Use: Pavlovas are frequently made at home for special events such as Christmas and birthdays, appreciated for their light texture and colorful toppings.

Sanga

- Meaning: A casual term for "sandwich," commonly used in informal discussions.
- Cultural Context: Reflecting Australia's tendency to shorten words, "sanga" is a more concise version of "sandwich."
- Example Usage: "I've packed a couple of sangas of ham and cheese for lunch."

- Tips for Use: Whether it's a simple peanut butter sanga or a gourmet creation, this term is widely used in everyday conversation.

Schnitty

- Meaning: An abbreviation for "schnitzel," which is a breaded and fried meat cutlet, usually made from chicken or beef.
- Cultural Context: Australians adopted this German dish and added their flair, turning it into a popular pub meal.
- Example Usage: "The schnitty here is legendary, try it with some chips!"
- Tips for Use: Schnittys are typically accompanied by gravy, salad, or lemon wedges, making for a filling and enjoyable dish.

Smoko

- Meaning: A break during work, typically accompanied by tea, coffee, or snacks.
- Cultural Context: The term comes from "smoke-o," which initially described breaks when workers would step out for a quick cigarette. It has since expanded to refer to any brief pause during the workday.

- Example Usage: "We'll take smoko at 10 AM. Grab something to eat if you're hungry."
- Tips for Use: Smoko is a valued custom in Australian workplaces, providing an opportunity to unwind and rejuvenate.

Snag

- Meaning: A colloquial term for "sausage," commonly found at barbecues and sports events.
- Cultural Context: This word highlights the significance of sausages in Australian food culture, particularly at outdoor events.
- Example Usage: "Don't forget to grab some snags for the Barbie tonight!"

- Tips for Use: Snags are available in various types, including traditional beef and spicy chorizo, and are typically served with bread, onions, and ketchup, often referred to as "dead horse."

Snot Block

- Meaning: A colloquial term for a vanilla slice, which is a pastry dessert filled with custard and covered in icing.
- Cultural Context: The whimsical name probably comes from its similarity to a lump of mucus, but it tastes much better!
- Example Usage: "If you've got a sweet tooth, try the snot block. It's divine!"
- Tips for Use: Although its name may sound off-putting, the snot block is a popular dessert found in bakeries and cafes throughout Australia.

Tucker

- Meaning: A broad term for food, commonly used in casual or rural contexts.
- Cultural Context: Derived from old English slang, "tucker" became associated with food in Australia, especially among bushmen and travelers.
- Example Usage: "Let's dig into some tucker; it's been a long day!"
- Tips for Use: This term is often heard at campsites, roadhouses, or any place where people come together to eat.

Chapter 3:
Nature & Outdoors

Australia's vast landscapes offer countless opportunities for adventure, but understanding the local terminology is essential for navigating the terrain! In this section, you'll discover words associated with the outdoors, such as "Roos" (Kangaroos) and "Mozzies" (Mosquitoes). Whether you're trekking through the "Bush," swimming in a "Rockhole," or relaxing by a "Fair dinkum fire," these expressions will help you convey your experiences authentically. Get ready to immerse yourself in Australia's breathtaking nature while mastering its unique language.

Arvo

- Meaning: A colloquial term for "afternoon," commonly used when organizing outdoor events or informal meet-ups.
- Cultural Context: The Australian culture is known for shortening words, and "arvo" exemplifies this habit.
- Example Usage: "Let's head out for a bushwalk in the arvo. It'll be nice and cool."

- Tips for Use: The term "arvo" can be used for any afternoon plans, particularly those related to nature or leisure.

Billabong

- Meaning: A still body of water or pond, typically created when a river alters its path.
- Cultural Context: The term comes from an Aboriginal word that translates to "backwater," and billabongs are well-known elements of Australia's countryside.
- Example Usage: "We took a break at a billabong on our road trip. It was an ideal location for taking pictures."
- Tips for Use: Billabongs serve as refuges for various wildlife, such as birds and fish, which makes them favored spots for nature lovers.

Bogged

- Meaning: Trapped in mud or sand, typically used to describe vehicles in off-road situations.
- Cultural Context: The term highlights the difficulties of traversing Australia's rough landscapes, where soft soil can easily ensnare unprepared drivers.
- Example Usage: "The ute got bogged in the creek bed. We had to call for help!"
- Tips for Use: When venturing into isolated regions, it's essential to have recovery equipment on hand to prevent getting bogged, and be sure to seek guidance from locals!.

Brumby

- Meaning: A wild horse commonly located in the mountainous areas of Australia.
- Cultural Context: Brumbies are the descendants of domestic horses that either escaped or were left behind, and they have come to represent freedom and strength.
- Example Usage: "On our hike, we spotted a herd of brumbies grazing near the ridge."
- Tips for Use: Although they are stunning creatures, brumbies can be contentious because of their effects on local ecosystems. Be sure to follow local regulations if you come across them.

Bush

- Meaning: This term denotes wild, forested, or rural regions, capturing the spirit of Australia's natural environments.
- Cultural Context: The word "bush" is deeply embedded in Australian culture, symbolizing both its beauty and the challenges it presents.
- Example Usage: "Let's go camping in the bush this weekend. It'll be great to disconnect from city life."

- Tips for Use: Venturing into the bush provides breathtaking views, but it's important to be well-prepared. Always monitor weather forecasts and pack necessary items like water and sunscreen.

Bush Tucker

- Meaning: Foods native to Australia that are gathered from the wild, including fruits, nuts, seeds, and animals.
- Cultural Context: Indigenous Australians have sustainably collected bush tucker for thousands of years, and it is now becoming increasingly popular among culinary enthusiasts.
- Example Usage: "During the tour, we learned about different types of bush tucker, like quandongs and witchetty grubs."
- Tips for Use: Sampling bush tucker offers a distinctive opportunity to engage with Australia's vibrant cultural history. It is advisable to participate in guided tours to identify which plants are safe for consumption.

Bushwalking

- Meaning: The activity of hiking or trekking in natural settings, typically in forests, mountains, or along coastlines.
- Cultural Context: Bushwalking is a popular activity in Australia, providing an opportunity for individuals to discover various landscapes while remaining physically active.
- Example Usage: "Yesterday, we went bushwalking in the national park, and it was stunning!"

- Tips for Use: Whether you opt for a brief walk or an extended journey, bushwalking allows you to connect with nature. Be sure to wear durable footwear and bring sufficient water.

Chuck a U-ie

- Meaning: Execute a swift U-turn, often used in a lighthearted manner while driving, particularly in countryside settings.
- Cultural Context: This expression reflects the spontaneity of road trips and the necessity for adaptability when driving in rural areas.
- Example Usage: "Oh no, we missed the turnoff. Let's chuck a U-ie before we go too far!"
- Tips for Use: In certain locations, making a U-turn may be prohibited due to traffic regulations or road circumstances, so it's important to remain vigilant.

Creek

- Meaning: A creek is a minor river or stream, frequently found in outdoor activities.
- Cultural Context: Creeks play a vital role in Australia's environment, serving as water sources for both animals and people.
- Example Usage: "We navigated across multiple creeks on our hike, which made it more challenging!"
- Tips for Use: Numerous creeks may dry up in times of drought, so it's important not to depend on them for drinking water unless it has been properly treated.

Drought Breaker

- Meaning: Rain that concludes an extended dry period, providing relief to both farmers and natural ecosystems.
- Cultural Context: In Australia, drought breakers are significant occurrences, as extended dry spells can greatly affect agriculture and local communities.
- Example Usage: "At last, we experienced a real drought breaker last night; the fields are absorbing the rain!"
- Tips for Use: When visiting rural regions during a drought, locals will be grateful if you mention your hopes for rain!

Dunny

- Meaning: A toilet located outside, commonly seen in camping sites or isolated areas.
- Cultural Context: This term captures the practical essence of outdoor living, where amenities are simple yet functional.
- Example Usage: "The dunny at the campsite wasn't glamorous, but it did the job."
- Tips for Use: When utilizing a dunny, adhere to Leave No Trace guidelines to maintain a clean and unspoiled environment.

Fair Dinkum Fire

- Meaning: A genuine campfire, usually created for warmth, cooking, or sharing stories.
- Cultural Context: The term merges "fair dinkum" (meaning genuine) with "fire," highlighting its authenticity and traditional roots.
- Example Usage: "We started a fair dinkum fire beneath the stars; it was enchanting."
- Tips for Use: When constructing a campfire, it's important to be mindful and respectful of the environment. Always verify fire regulations and ensure fires are fully extinguished before departing.

Gidgee

- Meaning: A resilient, small tree that originates from the dry areas of Australia is recognized for its ability to withstand extreme conditions.
- Cultural Context: The gidgee tree flourishes in arid climates, playing a vital role in the ecosystem of desert regions.
- Example Usage: "While driving through the outback, we noticed several gidgee trees. They are incredibly tough!"
- Tips for Use: The wood of the gidgee tree is valued for its strength and is occasionally utilized in making tools or furniture.

Goanna

- Meaning: A sizable monitor lizard found in Australia, frequently observed sunbathing or searching for food.

- Cultural Context: Goannas are emblematic of Australia's natural environment and are essential for ecosystem balance.
- Example Usage: "Be on the lookout for goannas during your hike; they tend to be quite inquisitive!"
- Tips for Use: Although they are mostly harmless, goannas can protect themselves if they feel threatened, so it's best to appreciate them from a safe distance.

Gum Tree

- Meaning: A type of eucalyptus tree, which is a well-known emblem of Australia's scenery.
- Cultural Context: There are more than 700 species of gum trees, which are prevalent in Australian woodlands and serve as homes for animals such as koalas and kookaburras.
- Example Usage: "The scent of the air was refreshing beneath the gum trees; it was truly a moment of relaxation."
- Tips for Use: The leaves of gum trees have oil that releases a unique fragrance, particularly following rainfall.

Humpy

- Meaning: A makeshift shelter constructed from bark and branches, commonly utilized by Aboriginal Australians.
- Cultural Context: Humpies were functional homes that could be assembled rapidly for brief periods, showcasing the ingenuity of Indigenous cultures.
- Example Usage: "During the tour, we discovered how to create a humpy with natural resources."
- Tips for Use: Constructing a humpy offers a practical way to engage with Australia's vibrant cultural history.

Kangaroo Court

- Meaning: A casual assembly or mock trial, typically associated with fun outdoor activities.
- Cultural Context: The term comes from the concept of spontaneous decision-making,

with kangaroo courts being playful courts organized among friends.
- Example Usage: "While camping, we set up a kangaroo court to determine who would be responsible for washing the dishes next!"
- Tips for Use: These events are intended to be entertaining and lighthearted, rather than serious legal matters.

Mizzle

- Meaning: A light, misty rain, typically referred to as a gentle drizzle.
- Cultural Context: The term "mizzle" comes from British slang and refers to weather frequently experienced in coastal regions.
- Example Usage: "This morning there was only a little mizzle, nothing to be concerned about!"
- Tips for Use: While a mizzle can make your clothes wet, it usually doesn't spoil an outdoor day.

Mozzie

- Meaning: A colloquial term for mosquito, a bothersome insect commonly found in Australia.
- Cultural Context: Australians abbreviated "mosquito" to "mozzie," showcasing their penchant for shortening words.
- Example Usage: "Make sure to bring repellent; the mozzies are aggressive around the waterholes!"

- Tips for Use: Mozzies are not only irritating; they can transmit diseases, so it's important to take safety measures.

Never-Never

- Meaning: Extremely remote outback areas, far from civilization.
- Cultural Context: This term evokes the isolation and vastness of Australia's interior.
- Example Usage: "Exploring the never-never requires careful planning. you're truly on your own out there."
- Tips for Use: Use this phrase to describe places where modern conveniences are scarce.

Outback

- Meaning: The outback refers to the remote and thinly populated interior areas of Australia, known for their rough terrain and distinctive wildlife.
- Cultural Context: The outback is considered the core of Australia, embodying themes of adventure and strength.
- Example Usage: "Visiting the outback is an experience you won't forget; just ensure you're well-prepared!"
- Tips for Use: Exploring the outback requires respect for nature and an understanding of safety measures.

Paperbark Tree

- Meaning: A type of tree characterized by its shedding bark, typically located in wetland regions.
- Cultural Context: Paperbark trees flourish in swampy habitats and derive their name from their thin, paper-like outer bark.
- Example Usage: "As we wandered through a grove of paperbark trees, it felt as if we had entered a different realm."
- Tips for Use: Their unique look makes paperbark trees easily recognizable while hiking in the bush.

Ripper

- Meaning: A term meaning outstanding, frequently used to refer to wonderful outdoor adventures.

- Cultural Context: This lively expression captures the thrill of discovering Australia's natural landscapes.
- Example Usage: "That sunrise hike was a ripper; it's a memory we'll cherish forever!"
- Tips for Use: The word "ripper" can be used to convey enthusiasm or appreciation for anything remarkable.

Rockhole

- Meaning: A natural pool of water in rocky terrain, often found in desert regions.
- Cultural Context: Rockholes are vital water sources for both humans and animals in arid areas.
- Example Usage: "We swam in a rockhole during our trek. it was refreshing and serene."
- Tips for Use: Always check water quality before swimming.

Roo

- Meaning: Short for "kangaroo," Australia's national emblem and most famous marsupial.
- Cultural Context: Kangaroos are deeply ingrained in Australian culture and identity.
- Example Usage: "Be careful driving at dusk. the roos are active then!"

- Tips for Use: Spotting a roo in the wild is a quintessential Australian experience.

Salty

- Meaning: A colloquial term for the saltwater crocodile, a top predator in Australia.
- Cultural Context: Salty crocodiles are found in estuaries and coastal areas, evoking both admiration and wariness.
- Example Usage: "Keep your distance from the riverbanks; we want to avoid encountering any salts!"
- Tips for Use: It's important to respect the territory of saltwater crocodiles and maintain a safe distance, as they are formidable animals.

Sandgroper

- Meaning: A term used to refer to individuals from Western Australia, named after a local insect.
- Cultural Context: Sandgropers are tiny insects that dig into sandy ground, similar to how early settlers adjusted to the conditions.
- Example Usage: "I'm traveling west to see my cousin; she's a proud sandgroper!"
- Tips for Use: People from Western Australia embrace this nickname, taking pride in their distinct identity.

Southerly Buster

- Meaning: A chilly wind that comes from the south, typically providing a welcome break from high temperatures.
- Cultural Context: This term is frequently used in eastern Australia, especially in New South Wales, to refer to abrupt decreases in temperature.
- Example Usage: "The southerly buster hit just in time. We needed that cool breeze!"
- Tips for Use: Although they are refreshing, southerly busters can also bring rain, so be sure to bring waterproof clothing if you're outside.

Stock Route

- Meaning: A designated path for moving livestock across rural areas, historically vital for agriculture.

- Cultural Context: Stock routes allowed drovers to transport cattle and sheep over long distances while accessing water and grazing land.
- Example Usage: "We followed an old stock route during our road trip, it felt like stepping back in time."
- Tips for Use: Many stock routes have been preserved for their historical significance and scenic beauty.

Swag

- Meaning: A mobile bedroll designed for camping, commonly preferred by explorers and travelers.
- Cultural Context: Swags were first used by swagmen (nomadic laborers) and continue to be a favorite among contemporary campers.
- Example Usage: "After pitching my tent, I decided to sleep under the stars in my trusty swag."

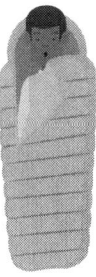

- Tips for Use: Using a swag provides an authentic outback experience, linking you to Australia's adventurous history.

Thongs

- Meaning: A colloquial term for flip-flops, ideal for relaxed outings or beach trips.
- Cultural Context: Australians enjoy wearing thongs due to their ease and comfort in warm climates.
- Example Usage: "Don't forget to bring your thongs; they're perfect for strolling on hot sand."
- Tips for Use: Be careful not to mix up this term with its other definitions in different contexts!

Top End

- Meaning: This term refers to the northern part of Australia, encompassing the Northern Territory and Far North Queensland.
- Cultural Context: The term "Top End" is used to describe the tropical and subtropical areas recognized for their breathtaking scenery and distinctive wildlife.
- Example Usage: "We're planning to visit the Top End next year to explore Kakadu National Park."
- Tips for Use: The Top End features attractions such as rivers teeming with crocodiles, verdant rainforests, and striking gorges.

Tucker Bag

- Meaning: A bag or container used for carrying food during outdoor trips, ensuring supplies stay organized.
- Cultural Context: Tucker bags have been essential companions for bushwalkers, campers, and travelers since early settlement.
- Example Usage: "Before heading out, I packed the tucker bag with snacks and sandwiches."
- Tips for Use: Modern versions include backpacks and esky-style coolers for keeping perishables fresh.

Wattle

- Meaning: The acacia tree, recognized as Australia's national floral symbol, is famous for its bright yellow blossoms.
- Cultural Context: Wattles flourish abundantly throughout Australia and represent strength and togetherness.
- Example Usage: "During spring, the wattles transform the hills into a stunning golden landscape!"
- Tips for Use: Wattle Day, observed on September 1st, pays tribute to this significant plant.

Willy-Willy

- Meaning: A small tornado or dust devil that typically appears swirling over arid terrains.
- Cultural Context: The term was coined by Aboriginal Australians to describe these occurrences, which happen when warm air ascends quickly.
- Example Usage: "Watch out for willy-willies on the plain, they can kick up quite a fuss!"
- Tips for Use: Generally harmless, willy-willies can bring excitement to otherwise calm environments.

Wombat

- Meaning: A compact, burrowing marsupial found in Australia, recognized for its robust physique and nighttime activity.
- Cultural Context: Wombats are cherished for their unique behaviors and their significant contribution to ecosystem dynamics.
- Example Usage: "We saw a wombat close to its burrow at sunrise. It was so cute!"
- Tips for Use: Maintain a safe distance when watching wombats, as they may act aggressively if they feel threatened.

Woop Woop

- Meaning: A playful term for distant or rural locations, typically used in a humorous context.
- Cultural Context: Woop Woop conveys the notion of a place that is remote or of little importance.
- Example Usage: "Where do you live?" "Just out in Woop Woop!"
- Tips for Use: This expression is best used in a light-hearted manner when talking about less-traveled areas.

Yabby

- Meaning: A type of freshwater crayfish that is commonly harvested for food during outdoor excursions.

- Cultural Context: Yabbies are simple to catch with nets or baited traps, which makes them a popular activity for families.
- Example Usage: "How about we go yabbying at the creek? It's enjoyable for all!"
- Tips for Use: Preparing and cooking freshly caught yabbies is a tasty way to appreciate the gifts of nature.

Yakka

- Meaning: Refers to strenuous work, particularly linked to outdoor physical labor.
- Cultural Context: The term comes from an Aboriginal word that translates to "work," highlighting the importance of hard work and dedication.
- Example Usage: "Putting up the fence was yakka, but we managed to finish it on schedule."

- Tips for Use: Yakka is commonly used to characterize activities that demand physical strength and resolve.

Zebra Finch

- Meaning: A small bird found in grasslands and open forests, recognized for its vibrant feathers and joyful song.
- Cultural Context: Zebra finches are widely kept as pets around the globe, yet they flourish in the varied environments of Australia.
- Example Usage: "As we wandered through the reserve, we heard the cheerful chirping of zebra finches."
- Tips for Use: Their unique patterns and energetic calls make zebra finches easily recognizable.

Chapter 4: Socializing & Culture

Australians take great pleasure in engaging in friendly conversations over or a "Shout" (a round of drinks). This chapter equips you with the skills to socialize like a local, including how to offer a "Mate's rate" and avoid being labeled a "Knocker" (critic) and even partake in light-hearted teasing with "Taking the piss." By the end of this chapter, you'll be ready to participate in lively discussions and genuinely connect with those you meet.

Aussie Salute

- Meaning: The act of swatting flies away from your face, often seen in rural or outdoor environments.
- Cultural Context: During the warmer months, the presence of flies can be bothersome, resulting in this distinctive hand-waving action.
- Example Usage: "After an hour outside, I mastered my Aussie salute!"

- Tips for Use: This lighthearted term emphasizes the practicality of living in Australia's sunnier areas.

Chook Raffle

- Meaning: A fundraising raffle typically organized at pubs or community gatherings, where prizes can include chickens or various other items.
- Cultural Context: Chook raffles serve as a fun method to generate funds for local initiatives while fostering community spirit.
- Example Usage: "We won a chook raffle last week and ended up bringing home some eggs!"
- Tips for Use: Keep in mind that the term "chook" may not always refer to an actual chicken; the focus is more on enjoyment and community bonding.

Dinki Di

- Meaning: Refers to something or someone genuine or authentic, particularly about Australian culture.
- Cultural Context: This term probably has its origins in Aboriginal languages and

signifies trustworthiness and sincerity.

- Example Usage: "That guy is as dinki di as they get; you can count on him."

- Tips for Use: The phrase "dinki di" can be used to commend the authenticity or sincerity of individuals and experiences alike.

Fair Dinkum

- Meaning: Sincerely; genuinely, used to stress honesty or truth.

- Cultural Context: A fundamental part of Australian slang, "fair dinkum" represents principles such as fairness and integrity.

- Example Usage: "Is it fair dinkum that kangaroos fight with man? I need to witness it myself!"

- Tips for Use: This expression is ideal for conveying authentic curiosity or consensus in discussions.

Footy

- Meaning: A colloquial term for Australian Rules Football or Rugby, which are among the most favored sports in Australia.

- Cultural Context: Australians often shorten "football" to "footy," showcasing their enthusiasm for sports.

- Example Usage: "Tonight's footy match is significant. Be sure to catch it!"

- Tips for Use: The culture surrounding footy is strong in Australia, characterized by dedicated fans and vibrant traditions on match days.

Give It a Go

- Meaning: A phrase used to encourage someone to attempt something unfamiliar, typically in a casual or social context.
- Cultural Context: This expression embodies the adventurous nature of Australians, who appreciate effort and involvement.
- Example Usage: "Haven't gone bushwalking yet? Give it a go; it's excellent exercise"
- Tips for Use: This phrase can be used to inspire others or demonstrate a readiness to take on new experiences.

Hard Yakka

- Meaning: Refers to strenuous work, especially physical labor or challenging tasks.
- Cultural Context: The term "hard yakka" comes from Aboriginal languages and highlights the values of determination and commitment.
- Example Usage: "Constructing that fence was hard yakka, but we completed it!"
- Tips for Use: This phrase can be used to recognize effort or to describe tasks that are tough but ultimately fulfilling.

How're Ya Goin'?

- Meaning: A friendly way to ask "How are you?" or "How's everything?"
- Cultural Context: This expression reflects the informal and straightforward style of communication commonly found in Australia.
- Example Usage: "G'day mate, how're ya going today with work'?"
- Tips for Use: You can reply with "Not bad, thanks" or provide a brief update to continue the chat.

Kick-Ons

- Meaning: Extending a celebration or night out at a different venue after the primary event concludes.
- Cultural Context: Kick-ons embody the relaxed and spontaneous social culture of Australians.

- Example Usage: "Since the bar shut down early, we went to a friend's house for kick-ons."
- Tips for Use: Get ready for unplanned meet-ups and late-night enjoyment when participating in kick-ons!

Knackered

- Meaning: Feeling very tired or worn out, typically used after a long day or night of activities.
- Cultural Context: The term probably originates from old English slang referring to horses that were worn out, and it is now commonly used in Australia.
- Example Usage: "I was completely knackered after dancing all night!"

- Tips for Use: A great way to humorously or relatably express exhaustion.

Knock Off

- Meaning: To complete work or cease an activity, typically followed by socializing or taking a break.
- Cultural Context: The term "knocking off" indicates the conclusion of a job or work period, allowing for free time.
- Example Usage: "I knock off at 5 PM, so let's go for a coffee afterward!"
- Tips for Use: Use "knock off" in conjunction with plans to relax or commemorate the end of the day.

Laid-Back

- Meaning: Characterized by a relaxed and easygoing demeanor, reflecting the common social attitude in Australia.
- Cultural Context: This term embodies the spirit of Australian culture, highlighting a sense of tranquility and flexibility.
- Example Usage: "Australians tend to be quite laid-back regarding beach dress codes"
- Tips for Use: Adopting a laid-back attitude can help you blend in effortlessly with locals while traveling.

Legend

- Meaning: A person who is commendable or supportive, frequently used as a compliment in informal situations.
- Cultural Context: In Australian culture, legends refer to renowned individuals, and the term also applies to ordinary heroes.
- Example Usage: "I appreciate you giving me a ride. You're a legend!"
- Tips for Use: Referring to someone as a "legend" conveys gratitude and admiration for their behavior or character.

Mate's Rates

- Meaning: Reduced prices provided to friends or acquaintances.
- Cultural Context: Represents the importance Australians place on friendship and mutual support.
- Example Usage: "I purchased this painting at mate's rates from my neighbor; he's an amazing artist!"
- Tips for Use: Use "mate's rates" when discussing or negotiating special offers among friends.

No Dramas

- Meaning: A casual way to say that there's no issue; don't stress about it.
- Cultural Context: Australians tend to favor a relaxed and easygoing approach, which is why "no dramas" is frequently used as a reply.

- Example Usage: "Apologies for my tardiness!" "No dramas, mate."
- Tips for Use: This expression is useful for easing tension and demonstrating empathy in social interactions.

Shout

- Meaning: To treat a group to drinks, usually during social gatherings or celebrations.
- Cultural Context: The practice of shouting rounds is a tradition that promotes friendship and sharing among companions.
- Example Usage: "It's my shout; what would you like?"
- Tips for Use: It's important to return the favor if someone buys you a drink; this is part of the etiquette with people.

Skite

- Meaning: To brag or flaunt, which is generally frowned upon in Australian culture that values humility.
- Cultural Context: Skiting goes against the principles of fairness and equality, which are fundamental in Australia.
- Example Usage: "He spent the whole evening skiting about his new car, and it became quite irritating."
- Tips for Use: While light-hearted teasing is acceptable, too much boasting can drive people away.

Sober as a Judge

- Meaning: Fully sober, typically used in a lighthearted manner to highlight clarity or self-control.
- Background: This expression likens being sober to the seriousness and neutrality that judges are expected to maintain.
- Example Usage: "I'm driving tonight, so I'll have to stay sober as a judge."
- Extra Information: This phrase can be used to justify your decision to refrain from drinking in specific circumstances.

Stirrer

- Meaning: A person who incites trouble or conflict, often playfully or cheekily.
- Cultural Context: Stirrers enjoy engaging in playful conversations and like to ignite discussions or humor.
- Example Usage: "Ignore him; he's just a stirrer looking to provoke a reaction from you."
- Tips for Use: Being labeled a stirrer can have a positive connotation, particularly when it's all in good fun.

Straya

- Meaning: A colloquial term for "Australia," pronounced with an elongated vowel sound ("Straya").
- Cultural Context: This abbreviation is a representation of Australian phonetic humor and has gained iconic status.
- Example Usage: "Welcome to Straya! Make sure you have your sunscreen handy!"

- Tips for Use: Incorporating "Straya" into discussions and writing gives a bit of local character.

Taking the Piss

- Meaning: Light-heartedly teasing or ridiculing someone in a friendly manner, without any intent to harm.
- Cultural Context: This humorous expression is commonly found in Australian conversations and is a key part of their playful banter.
- Example Usage: "I was just taking the piss; you know I wasn't being serious!"
- Tips for Use: Keep your tone friendly to prevent any offense during these playful interactions.

True Blue

- Meaning: A term that signifies being genuinely Australian, referring to a person or thing that truly embodies the culture.
- Cultural Context: The phrase "true blue" reflects values such as loyalty, honesty, and authenticity, which are highly regarded in Australian culture.
- Example Usage: "That guy is as true blue as they get, you can rely on him whenever you need."

- Tips for Use: This expression can be used to commend someone's dependability or their ties to Australian customs.

Tucker Box

- Meaning: A receptacle designed for transporting food, particularly during work or outdoor excursions.
- Cultural Context: Tucker boxes help keep meals fresh and orderly while on the go or working in remote locations.
- Example Usage: "Don't forget to pack the tucker box before we leave; it will save us time later."
- Tips for Use: Contemporary variations include lunchboxes and coolers, yet the fundamental idea remains unchanged.

Tuckshop

- Meaning: A small food service area or snack bar, typically located in schools or community centers.
- Cultural Context: Tuckshops provide quick meals and beverages, serving as social gathering places.
- Example Usage: "Let's meet at the tuckshop after class to get a snack."
- Tips for Use: These locations are ideal for socializing with friends or having a quick meal.

Whinge

- Meaning: To express dissatisfaction or complain, typically in a lighthearted or critical manner.
- Background: Whinging is considered unhelpful, leading Australians to advise against too much complaining.
- Sample Sentence: "Quit whinging about the long road; our destination is coming!"
- Extra Information: This word can be used to playfully poke fun at someone who is complaining excessively.

Yabbo

- Meaning: A slang term for someone rough or uncivilized, typically used in a lighthearted manner among friends.
- Cultural Context: This term comes from "yobbo," which refers to individuals who exhibit loud or rowdy behavior.
- Example Usage: "You can be such a yabbo at times, but that's what makes you lovable!"
- Tips for Use: It's important to consider the context; "yabbo" should be used in an affectionate way rather than as an insult.

Yeah Nah

- Meaning: A courteous way to decline or show uncertainty, blending both agreement and disagreement.
- Cultural Context: This expression reflects the relaxed style of communication typical in Australia.
- Example Usage: "Would you like to watch a movie?" "Yeah nah, I believe I'll head to bed."
- Tips for Use: It's a classic Australian method of saying "no thanks" while maintaining a friendly tone.

Chapter 5:
Travel & Transport

From "Ute" (Pickup truck) to "Road trains," Australian transport has its unique vocabulary. This chapter deciphers the slang you'll encounter while traveling, whether you're driving along a "Dirtie" (Dirt road), catching a ride with a "Cabbie" (Taxi driver), or marveling at a "Hook turn" in Melbourne. Understanding terms like "Rego" (Vehicle registration) will make planning trips smoother and interactions easier. Buckle up it's time to hit the road with confidence!

Arvo Run

- Meaning: A brief excursion or drive in the afternoon, typically for relaxation or errands.
- Cultural Context: The term merges "Arvo" (short for afternoon) with "Run," highlighting the laid-back style of travel in Australia.
- Example Usage: "Let's go for an arvo run to the beach. It'll be nice and cool."
- Tips for Use: The phrase "Arvo Run" is suitable for describing spontaneous outings that are easy to organize.

Back of Bourke

- Meaning: Refers to a very isolated area; often humorously used to denote far-off places.
- Cultural Context: The term comes from Bourke, a town in the remote region of New South Wales, and has become a part of Australian slang representing seclusion.
- Example Usage: "Their farm is way out in the back of Bourke. You'll need a good map to find it!"

- Tips for Use: This expression enhances descriptions of distant locations or difficult-to-navigate areas.

Bail Out

- Meaning: To swiftly leave a vehicle, commonly used in casual situations.
- Cultural Context: This term comes from aviation language ("bailing out" of an aircraft) and has been adapted for use with cars and other types of vehicles.

- Example Usage: "We needed to bail out of the car when we noticed the flat tire."
- Tips for Use: Although it is primarily used in a figurative sense, it can also pertain to jumping out in urgent situations. Use it appropriately!

Bingle

- Meaning: A small car accident, usually resulting in minor scratches or dents.
- Cultural Context: Probably a shortened form of "collision," bingles are frequent occurrences but seldom serious.
- Example Usage: "I had a minor bingle at the roundabout, but it's nothing to worry about."
- Tips for Use: There's no need to stress if you hear about a bingle; they can typically be resolved with little trouble.

Bitumen

- Meaning: Asphalt or paved roads, often called "the bitumen" by travelers.
- Cultural Context: Australians use the term "bitumen" to differentiate between paved roads and unpaved paths.
- Example Usage: "We spent hours on unpaved roads before getting back on the bitumen."
- Tips for Use: Sticking to bitumen roads provides a smoother travel experience compared to rougher surfaces.

Bonnet

- Meaning: The cover of a car's engine compartment.
- Cultural Context: The Australian automotive language is influenced by British English.
- Example Usage: "The mechanic opened the bonnet to diagnose the engine issue."
- Tips for Use: This term is used when someone has an engine issue and his car.

Boot

- Meaning: The storage compartment at the back of a car, utilized for holding luggage or other items.
- Cultural Context: This term is an instance of British English that has been adopted in Australia.
- Example Usage: "Don't forget to put everything in the boot before we head out."
- Tips for Use: Similar to "bonnet," the term "boot" might be perplexing for those outside Australia who are not familiar with local car lingo.

Bottler

- Meaning: A remarkable trip or experience, focusing on high quality and enjoyment.
- Cultural Context: The term "bottler" embodies the optimistic spirit Australians have towards their adventures and travels.
- Example Usage: "That drive to the coast was truly a bottler; we'll cherish it for a lifetime!"
- Tips for Use: Use "bottler" to emphasize exceptional moments in your travels.

Bush Bash

- Meaning: Driving off-road in rough terrain, typically linked to adventure and exploration.
- Cultural Context: Bush-bashing entails maneuvering through difficult landscapes, which challenges the driver's abilities and the vehicle's strength.
- Example Usage: "We went bush bashing last weekend, it was exciting but tiring!"
- Tips for Use: It's important to be well-prepared for bush bashes with the right equipment, fuel, and understanding of the location.

Cabbie

- Meaning: A taxi driver, is commonly used in Australian slang.
- Cultural Context: A shortened form of "cab driver," cabbies are essential for city transportation.
- Example Usage: "The cabbie drove us directly to the hotel, even with the heavy traffic."

- Tips for Use: Cabbies frequently act as informal tour guides, providing local insights about their cities.

Camper Trailer

- Meaning: A mobile trailer intended for camping and travel, offering comfort and ease.
- Cultural Context: Camper trailers have become vital for extended journeys through Australia's expansive terrains.
- Example Usage: "We rented a camper trailer for our vacation; it simplified our experience!"

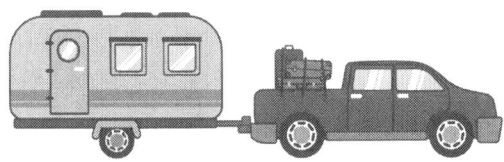

- Tips for Use: Ideal for adventure enthusiasts who want to explore while still enjoying modern conveniences.

Chockers

- Meaning: Filled to the brim, typically used to refer to crowded areas such as roads or event spaces.
- Cultural Context: The term "chockers" conveys the feeling of being inundated by a large amount or high density.
- Example Usage: "The highway was chockers with visitors during the busy season."
- Tips for Use: This word can be applied to various situations, including traffic congestion and lively marketplaces.

Cooee

- Meaning: A shout used to draw attention from afar, often humorously referenced about navigation difficulties.
- Cultural Context: This term originated from an Aboriginal call, known for its ability to carry sound over large areas.q

- Example Usage: "If you happen to lose your way, just shout, I'll be within cooee distance!"
- Tips for Use: Although not commonly used in modern times, "cooee" serves as a lighthearted reference to old-fashioned ways of communicating.

Dirtie

- Meaning: A type of unpaved or dirt road commonly found in rural or remote regions.
- Cultural Context: This term is a shortened form of "dirt road," showcasing Australia's fondness for abbreviations.
- Example Usage: "The final part of our trip was on a dirtie, and it was quite bumpy!"

- Tips for Use: Caution is needed when driving on dirt roads, particularly after rainfall, as they can become slick.

Driveway

- Meaning: A personal road that provides access to a residence or property, typically utilized for parking vehicles.
- Cultural Context: Widely used in English-speaking nations, the term "driveway" continues to be significant in Australian suburbs.
- Example Usage: "Please park in the driveway while we collect our bags."
- Tips for Use: The dimensions and state of driveways can differ greatly based on the area.

Fair Dinkum Road

- Meaning: A lengthy, straight road, often used in a humorous context to depict perfect driving conditions.
- Cultural Context: Merges the term "fair dinkum" (meaning genuine) with the idea of an ideal road, symbolizing a positive outlook on travel.
- Example Usage: "This road is a fair dinkum road, with no bends for miles!"
- Tips for Use: This phrase can be used playfully to commend smooth and uncomplicated trips.

Flat Tyre

- Meaning: A tire that has been punctured and needs to be fixed or replaced before you can continue your journey.
- Cultural Context: In Australia, the term "flat tyre" is preferred over "flat tire," following British spelling rules.
- Example Usage: "We encountered a flat tyre midway through our journey, but fortunately, there was a service station close by."
- Tips for Use: It's important to have a spare tire and necessary tools when traveling in isolated regions.

Footpath

- Meaning: A walkway for pedestrians located next to roads in city and suburban environments.
- Cultural Context: This term reflects the influence of British English on the Australian language.
- Example Usage: "Be cautious of cyclists on the footpath, as they may not always adhere to regulations."
- Tips for Use: In certain older towns, footpaths can be quite narrow, so it's important to remain vigilant while walking.

Freeway

- Meaning: A highway or motorway designed for faster, uninterrupted travel between cities or regions.
- Cultural Context: Freeways connect major population centers and are crucial for long-distance travel.
- Example Usage: "We'll take the freeway to avoid traffic, it's quicker that way."
- Tips for Use: Observe speed limits and rest regularly during freeway drives to stay safe.

Give Way

- Meaning: Yield, meaning that drivers are required to let others go first at intersections.
- Cultural Context: A component of Australia's traffic regulations and road signs, highlighting the importance of safety and politeness.
- Example Usage: "A give way sign is coming up, reduce your speed and look out for other vehicles."
- Tips for Use: Knowing how to interpret "give way" signs is crucial for safe driving on Australian roads.

Gnarly

- Meaning: Difficult, frequently used to refer to roads or driving situations.
- Cultural Context: Originally from surf culture, "gnarly" has evolved to describe anything challenging or demanding.
- Example Usage: "The dirt road was gnarly; we had to take it slow to prevent any damage."
- Tips for Use: This term is suitable for describing rough landscapes or complicated driving tasks.

Grey Nomads

- Meaning: Retired individuals who travel widely across Australia in campervans or vehicles, discovering various parts of the country.
- Cultural Context: Grey nomads represent a sense of adventure and independence, relishing life on the road.
- Example Usage: "You'll encounter numerous grey nomads at well-frequented camping locations; they have fascinating stories to tell!"
- Tips for Use: A lot of grey nomads participate in online groups to share travel tips and insights.

Hire Car

- Meaning: A rental vehicle, often utilized by travelers and residents for temporary transportation requirements.
- Cultural Context: Renting vehicles serves as a convenient option for discovering areas lacking dependable public transportation.
- Example Usage: "As we plan to visit several towns, we opted to hire a car for the week."
- Tips for Use: It's advisable to reserve rental vehicles ahead of time, particularly during busy seasons, to ensure availability.

Hook Turn

- Meaning: Melbourne's unique right-turn method for trams, where drivers turn left into a designated lane before completing the turn.
- Cultural Context: Designed to accommodate tram lines, hook turns are iconic to Melbourne's road system.
- Example Usage: "Be prepared for hook turns if you're driving in Melbourne, it takes some getting used to!"
- Tips for Use: Follow signs carefully when attempting hook turns to avoid confusion or fines.

Hostie

- Meaning: A colloquial term for flight attendant.
- Cultural Context: Hosties are essential for maintaining passenger comfort during air travel.
- Example Usage: "The hostie brought us snacks and drinks during the flight, which we appreciated."
- Tips for Use: While this term is commonly recognized in Australia, it may be puzzling for those from other countries.

How Ya Gonna Get There?

- Meaning: This informal phrase is a way of inquiring, "How will you arrive?" and is commonly used in discussions about planning.
- Cultural Context: It showcases the relaxed attitude Australians have towards travel and logistics.
- Example Usage: "What's your destination for tomorrow?" "Not sure yet, how ya gonna get there?"
- Tips for Use: This expression can be used to initiate conversations about different transportation methods or routes.

Jackaroo/Jillaroo

- Meaning: Young individuals employed on farms or stations, typically during their travels or gap year.
- Cultural Context: Jackaroos (males) and Jillaroos (females) acquire practical agricultural skills while engaging in outdoor activities.
- Example Usage: "Following university, I worked as a jackaroo in Queensland for a year, it was tough work but fulfilling."
- Tips for Use: Being a jackaroo or jillaroo is considered a significant experience for many young adventurers.

Main Drag

- Meaning: The primary street or road in a town, usually lively with various shops, cafes, and activities.
- Cultural Context: The term "drag" denotes the central pathway.
- Example Usage: "How about we go to the main drag for lunch? There's an excellent café there."

- Tips for Use: Visiting the main drag is an excellent way to enjoy the charm of a small town.

Milk Run

- Meaning: A brief, regular trip typically for errands or deliveries.
- Cultural Context: Originally related to milk delivery routes, the term has evolved to refer to any regular journey.
- Example Usage: "I'm just making a quick milk run to the grocery store, I'll return shortly!"
- Tips for Use: Milk runs are ideal for efficiently managing multiple tasks on hectic days.

Motorway

- Meaning: A primary road or expressway intended for quick, long-distance travel.
- Cultural Context: Motorways link citics and areas, providing effective transportation alternatives.
- Example Usage: "We'll use the motorway to bypass city traffic; it's faster that way."
- Tips for Use: Always verify road conditions and adhere to speed limits when traveling on motorways.

Old Bomb

- Meaning: A worn-out, unreliable vehicle, often lovingly called a "classic" by its owner.
- Cultural Context: Australians have a fondness for vintage cars, regardless of their condition.
- Example Usage: "My friend has an old bomb; it malfunctions more often than it actually works!"
- Tips for Use: This term is typically used in a lighthearted manner to refer to cars that have seen better days but are still cherished.

Outback Highway

- Meaning: Extensive roads that traverse isolated regions, linking distant towns and communities.
- Cultural Context: Outback highways serve as essential routes for rural Australia, facilitating travel over great distances.
- Example Usage: "The drive along the outback highway was amazing; we encountered kangaroos and beautiful scenery."
- Tips for Use: It's important to be well-prepared before embarking on journeys along outback highways, ensuring you have enough fuel, water, and emergency supplies.

Parked Up

- Meaning: Refers to being stopped or stationed in a place for a short time, commonly used to indicate parking.
- Cultural Context: Indicates a laid-back approach to making brief stops while traveling.
- Example Usage: "We parked up close to the beach and enjoyed the afternoon swimming."
- Tips for Use: The term "parked up" is ideal for highlighting informal, spontaneous stops along your travels.

Petrol

- Meaning: Gasoline, is the fuel used for vehicles, commonly referred to as "petrol" in Australia.
- Cultural Context: British English influence persists in Australian automotive vocabulary.
- Example Usage: "Make sure to fill up on petrol before heading into the outback, stations are few and far between."
- Tips for Use: Prices vary by region, so plan your refueling stops accordingly.

Rego

- Meaning: A term that stands for vehicle registration, which is mandatory for all vehicles on public roads.
- Cultural Context: The term "rego" is derived from the word "registration" and is a classic example of Australian slang.
- Example Usage: "Make sure to renew your rego before it runs out!"
- Tips for Use: Rego stickers or digital records should be visible or available for inspection.

Road Train

- Meaning: A very long truck commonly found in remote areas, made up of several trailers connected to one cab.
- Cultural Context: Road trains play a crucial role in moving goods over Australia's extensive distances.
- Example Usage: "Be cautious of road trains on the road; they can be daunting to overtake."
- Tips for Use: When passing road trains, ensure you provide them with ample space and time, as they are large and need careful maneuvering.

Roundabout

- Meaning: A circular traffic junction where cars travel in a counterclockwise direction around a central island.
- Cultural Context: Roundabouts help alleviate traffic congestion and enhance safety in comparison to conventional intersections.
- Example Usage: "Observe the signs at the roundabout to access the main street."
- Tips for Use: Always yield to vehicles that are already in the roundabout to prevent collisions.

Servo

- Meaning: A term for a service station, a place where you can refuel your car and purchase snacks or necessary items.
- Cultural Context: Servos are common throughout Australia, catering to both motorists and travelers.
- Example Usage: "We should stop at the next servo to take a break and pick up some snacks."

- Tips for Use: Numerous servos provide facilities such as restrooms, cafes, and convenience stores, making them perfect for quick stops.

Slushy

- Meaning: Refers to road conditions that are slippery or muddy, particularly following rainfall or in off-road situations.
- Cultural Context: This term highlights difficult driving surfaces that demand careful handling and expertise.

- Example Usage: "The path was slushy after the rain last night, so proceed with caution!"
- Tips for Use: It's advisable to refrain from driving on slushy roads unless needed, as they heighten the likelihood of accidents.

Speedo

- Meaning: Refers to either a speedometer (the instrument that measures a vehicle's speed) or a person who is very enthusiastic about speed.
- Cultural Context: The term has two meanings, making "speedo" adaptable in discussions.
- Example Usage: "Watch the speedo, you don't want to receive a ticket!" (Alternatively:) "He's such a speedo, he constantly drives his car at full throttle."
- Tips for Use: It's important to adhere to speed limits for safe driving.

Tarred Road

- Meaning: A paved roadway, as opposed to unpaved dirt or gravel paths found in rural regions.
- Cultural Context: Tarred roads offer a smoother ride and improved grip for vehicles.
- Example Usage: "As soon as we reached the tarred road, the ride was significantly more pleasant."
- Tips for Use: It's advisable to choose tarred roads for long trips unless you are prepared for more challenging surfaces.

Tinnie

- Meaning: A paved roadway, as opposed to unpaved dirt or gravel paths found in rural regions.
- Cultural Context: Tarred roads offer a smoother ride and improved grip for vehicles.
- Example Usage: "As soon as we reached the tarred road, the ride was significantly more pleasant."

- Example Usage: "We hired a tinnie for the day to fish in the river, it was awesome!"

- Tips for Use: Wear life jackets and follow boating regulations when using tinneys.

Track

- Meaning: An unpaved pathway often located in rural or remote regions that necessitates cautious driving.
- Cultural Context: Tracks are prevalent in the rough terrain of Australia, providing routes to secluded areas.
- Example Usage: "The map indicates a track that goes to the rock hole. Let's check if we can get through."
- Tips for Use: Make sure your vehicle is appropriate for tracks and bring recovery equipment if you plan to go off-road.

Ute

- Meaning: A utility vehicle akin to a pickup truck, commonly utilized for both work and recreational purposes.
- Cultural Context: Utes merge the functionality of a truck bed with the comfort of a passenger compartment.
- Example Usage: "A ute is ideal for transporting tools and camping equipment on road trips."

- Tips for Use: Utes are emblematic in Australia, symbolizing versatility and hard work.

Chapter 6:
Quirky & Funny Words

Welcome to the most entertaining aspect of Australian slang! This section will introduce you to the humorous and lighthearted expressions that Australians commonly use in their daily conversations. From playfully calling someone a "Galah" (meaning a fool or someone acting silly) to referring to a nosy individual as a "Sticky beak," these phrases will help you engage in casual chats with ease. Whether it's swimwear known as "Togs" or rowdy individuals referred to as "Yobbos," learning these terms will enhance the charm and authenticity of your interactions. Get ready to add some fun to your travels!

Bludger

- Meaning: A person who shirks work or responsibilities, is typically perceived as lazy or untrustworthy.
- Cultural Context: The term "bludger" probably comes from older slang referring to idle individuals or freeloaders, and it has evolved into a playful way to poke fun at those who are lazy.
- Example Usage: "Stop being a bludger and go complete your work!"

- Tips for Use: It's best to use this word in a lighthearted manner rather than in a serious tone to maintain a fun atmosphere.

Bogey Trap

- Meaning: A tissue box, whimsically referred to as a "bogey trap" due to its function of catching nasal mucus.
- Cultural Context: This amusing term merges usefulness with a hint of crude humor.
- Example Usage: "Could you hand me the bogey trap? I'm feeling a bit under the weather today."
- Tips for Use: Great for adding some levity during those sniffly times!

Chunder

- Meaning: A term for vomit, typically used in a lighthearted manner in informal discussions, though it can apply to more serious contexts as well.
- Cultural Context: Although it is a bit vulgar, "chunder" embodies the straightforward nature of Australian slang.
- Example Usage: (In a humorous way) "That spicy curry nearly made me chunder last night!"
- Tips for Use: Consider the context when using this word, as it may not be appropriate for every audience.

Dag

- Meaning: A person who is socially awkward yet lovable, often characterized as quirky or clumsy.
- Cultural Context: The term comes from sheep farming, where "dag" refers to the dried feces found around a sheep's tail, representing something untidy but innocuous.
- Example Usage: "You're such a dag for stumbling over your own feet like that!"
- Tips for Use: Calling someone a "dag" is not meant to be offensive; rather, it's a lighthearted tease about their charm or uniqueness.

Dunny Man

- Meaning: A person responsible for delivering portable toilets, playfully called the "Dunny Man."
- Cultural Context: The term merges "dunny" (a term for an outdoor toilet) with "man," resulting in a lighthearted job title.
- Example Usage: "The dunny man is on his way to prepare for the festival."
- Tips for Use: Incorporate this term to inject some humor into conversations about event planning.

Galah

- Meaning: A term for a fool or someone behaving foolishly, originating from the loud galah bird known for its raucous calls.
- Cultural Context: Galahs are vibrant parrots found in Australia, which led to this lighthearted insult.
- Example Usage: "He's a real galah, always cracking jokes at the wrong time."

- Tips for Use: Calling someone a "galah" is not intended to be offensive; it is typically used playfully.

Ginger Beer

- Meaning: A playful term for a person with red hair, often used lightheartedly among friends.
- Cultural Context: A fun combination of "ginger" (referring to redheads) and "beer" (a popular beverage), resulting in a humorous nickname.
- Example Usage: "Look over there, the ginger beer is waving at us!"
- Tips for Use: It's best to use this term in friendly situations, as some redheads may take offense if it's not said in a considerate way.

Groggy

- Meaning: A state of feeling tired or sluggish, often associated with the effects of drinking too much alcohol.

- Cultural Context: The term comes from "grog," which refers to alcoholic beverages, and it reflects the feeling one experiences after a night of drinking.
- Example Usage: "I feel kind of groggy this morning, had too many drinks last night!"
- Tips for Use: Groggy is a common term for those who have celebrated a bit too much.

Knocker

- Meaning: A person who harshly criticizes others, typically without providing helpful suggestions.
- Cultural Context: Represents the Australian principle of fairness and aims to reduce unwarranted negativity.
- Example Usage: "Stop being such a knocker; there's always potential for growth!"
- Tips for Use: This term can be used to playfully address overly critical attitudes.

Larrikin

- Meaning: A playful and cheeky individual who is endearing, typically linked to humor and a sense of playful defiance.
- Cultural Context: The term larrikin reflects the essence of enjoyment and nonconformity within Australian culture.
- Example Usage: "He's such a larrikin; he has a knack for making everyone laugh."
- Tips for Use: Being referred to as a larrikin is a positive remark, emphasizing your charisma and cleverness.

Mozzie Magnet

- Meaning: A term used humorously to refer to someone who draws in mosquitoes, often describing those who seem to attract bites.
- Cultural Context: The term merges "mozzie" (short for mosquito) with "magnet," playfully highlighting a person's tendency to get bitten.
- Example Usage: "You're such a mozzie magnet; we'll have to bring extra bug spray tonight!"
- Tips for Use: Great for joking with friends during outdoor activities or camping excursions.

Root Rat

- Meaning: A person who overindulges at a barbecue, frequently takes more food than they should.
- Cultural Context: Root rats are perceived as gluttonous or overly eager eaters, particularly during shared meals.
- Example Usage: "Be careful of the root rat; they'll gobble up all the sausages before anyone else has a chance!"
- Tips for Use: This term can be used in a lighthearted way to ensure that barbecues remain fair and fun for all attendees.

Spit the Dummy

- Meaning: To throw a fit or become very angry, often used in a humorous context to refer to exaggerated reactions.
- Cultural Context: This expression comes from the image of babies dropping their pacifiers in annoyance, reflecting similar outbursts in adults.
- Example Usage: "He really spat the dummy when he lost his money in the lottery."

- Tips for Use: This phrase is great for teasing about small outbursts while maintaining a playful tone.

Sticky Beak

- Meaning: A curious individual who tends to meddle in others' affairs, typically used humorously or playfully.
- Cultural Context: This lighthearted term comes from the idea of a bird with a sticky beak that investigates everything around it.
- Example Usage: "Why are you acting like such a sticky beak? Focus on your matters!"
- Tips for Use: When using this term in jest, make sure it's in a friendly tone to prevent hurting anyone's.

Togs

- Meaning: A term for swimwear that may seem outdated but remains popular in Australia.
- Cultural Context: The word "togs" brings back memories of previous beach outings, even with contemporary terms like "swimmers" or "bathers" in use.
- Example Usage: "Make sure to bring your togs if we go to the beach later!"

- Tips for Use: Use the unique term "togs" to infuse a bit of tradition into your discussions about the beach.

Yobbo

- Meaning: A rough or unrefined individual, typically used lightheartedly among friends to refer to someone with a relaxed demeanor.
- Cultural Context: Yobbos embody a carefree spirit and often disregard formal norms, which can make them charming in specific situations.
- Example Usage: "That guy is such a yobbo; he doesn't bother with all those fancy rules!"
- Tips for Use: It's important to consider the context; "yobbo" should be used in a friendly way rather than as an insult.

Zonked

- Meaning: Extremely tired or worn out, typically after a lengthy day or night of activities.
- Cultural Context: The term "zonked" captures the intense tiredness that results from overexertion.
- Example Usage: "I was completely zonked by the morning after dancing all night!"

- Tips for Use: This word can be used to convey a sense of profound fatigue in a lighthearted or relatable manner.

Chapter 7:
Witty Wisdom:
Aussie Idioms & Playful Phrases

Get ready to explore the essence of Australian humor! This chapter unveils a treasure trove of idioms and amusing expressions that showcase the country's flair for inventive communication. You'll encounter vibrant phrases such as "flat out like a lizard drinking" and "couldn't organize a piss-up in a brewery," each offering insight into the local culture and sense of humor. While some of these sayings may seem peculiar at first, they are all integral to the unique way Australians express themselves. By the end of this chapter, you'll possess insider knowledge that will enable you to impress locals and share a hearty laugh.

As Crook as Rookwood

- Meaning: Very sick or unwell.
- Cultural Context: Rookwood is a significant cemetery located in Sydney. Hence, the expression "as crook as Rookwood" playfully suggests that a person is as unwell as someone who is interred there. This is a quintessential instance of Australian dark humor.
- Example Usage: "After that flu hit me, I felt as crook as Rookwood!"

- Tips for Use: Playfully employ this phrase when referring to minor ailments or feeling unwell. Steer clear of using it in serious health-related contexts

As Keen as Barnacles on a Whale

- Meaning: Very enthusiastic or eager.
- Cultural Context: This expression likens enthusiasm to the strong grip barnacles have on whales, creating a striking and unique image that showcases the creativity of the Australian language.
- Example Usage: "He's as keen as barnacles on a whale to try his hand at surfing tomorrow!"
- Tips for Use: Ideal for characterizing someone who is excessively excited or resolute, particularly in fun or exaggerated situations.

Barking Up the Wrong Gum Tree

- Meaning: Misdirected effort or assumption.
- Cultural Context: Originating from the concept of dogs pursuing prey up the incorrect tree, this expression emphasizes the significance of remaining attentive and knowledgeable within Australian culture. It is frequently employed humorously to address someone's error.
- Example Usage: "If you think I'll lend you money, you're barking up the wrong gum tree!"
- Tips for Use: When using this phrase, approach it with care to highlight mistakes or misconceptions; it serves better as a playful correction rather than a severe reprimand.

Couldn't Find His Arse with Both Hands and a Map

- Meaning: Completely bewildered or disoriented.
- Cultural Context: This hyperbolic expression humorously highlights someone utterly lost or struggling to understand even the most basic situations.
- Example Usage: "If he thinks he'll find the Station Gasoil without GPS, he couldn't find his arse with both hands and a map!"
- Tips for Use: Employ this phrase in a lighthearted manner when referring to someone thoroughly confused; it works best in informal chats with friends.

Couldn't Organize a Piss-Up in a Brewery

- Meaning: Very chaotic or ineffective.
- Cultural Context: A brewery is a place for beer production, so if someone is unable to arrange a drinking event there, they must be quite incompetent. This expression reflects Australians' appreciation for self-mocking humor.
- Example Usage: "Don't ask him to plan the trip, he couldn't organize a piss-up in a brewery!"

- Tips for Use: Although humorous, this phrase may seem too blunt in some situations. Use it for playful teasing among friends or familiar people.

Don't Come the Raw Prawn with Me

- Meaning: Don't attempt to trick or mislead me.
- Cultural Context: The "raw prawn" analogy implies that someone is pretending to be different from their true self, similar to a raw prawn trying to appear cooked. It's a lighthearted way to highlight dishonesty.
- Example Usage: "You're telling me you didn't eat the last piece of pie? Don't come the raw prawn with me!"
- Tips for Use: This expression is ideal for situations where someone is lying or embellishing the truth; it's great for playful banter but may not be appropriate in formal contexts.

Flat Out Like a Lizard Drinking

- Definition: Very busy or working diligently.
- Cultural Context: This expression draws on the imagery of a lizard lying flat while sipping water, illustrating the idea of being stretched thin and concentrated.
- Example Usage: "I've been flat out like a lizard drinking all week; there's just so much to accomplish!"

- Tips for Use: Ideal for describing overwhelming tasks or busy schedules in a relatable and amusing manner.

Flogging a Dead Horse

- Meaning: Spending time on a hopeless cause.
- Cultural Context: This expression comes from the notion that beating a dead horse won't make it go, underscoring the futility of certain efforts. Australians often use it to point out inefficiency or obstinacy.
- Example Usage: "Attempting to repair that old car engine is like flogging a dead horse; we might as well get a new one."
- Tips for Use: Best used to convey annoyance over wasted efforts, particularly in problem-solving situations.

Got More Lies Than a Politician

- Meaning: Refers to a person who frequently tells untruths.
- Cultural Context: Australians enjoy teasing politicians, which makes this phrase a prime example of their clever humor. It amplifies the idea of dishonesty for comedic purposes.
- Example Usage: "He claims he's never late, but he's got more lies than a politician!"
- Tips for Use: Use this expression occasionally and in casual environments, as accusing someone of lying might be taken the wrong way depending on how it's said.

He'd Sell Sand to a Camel

- Meaning: Refers to someone who is extremely persuasive or deceitful in their sales tactics.
- Cultural Context: The idea of selling sand to a camel is ridiculous, highlighting the salesperson's skill in convincing anyone of anything. This expression showcases Australian appreciation for wit while also cautioning against being overly persuasive.
- Example Usage: "That bloke could sell ice to an Eskimo, he'd sell sand to a camel if given half the chance!"
- Tips for Use: Ideal for describing charismatic but unreliable individuals, like eager marketers or storytellers.

Keen as Mustard

- Meaning: Extremely enthusiastic.
- Cultural Context: Just as mustard enhances the taste of food, an enthusiastic individual injects vitality into any scenario. This expression playfully conveys eagerness.
- Example Usage: "She's keen as mustard to start her road trip tomorrow!"

- Tips for Use: Employ this phrase to characterize someone who is truly excited or driven; it carries a cheerful and playful tone.

Like a Frog in a Sock

- Meaning: Experiencing discomfort or awkwardness.
- Cultural Context: The image of a frog stuck in a sock effectively conveys a sense of unease. Australians enjoy playful language that creates unusual visuals.
- Example Usage: "Standing on stage was like being a frog in a sock for him, he just didn't know what to do!"
- Tips for Use: Ideal for describing feelings of discomfort or awkwardness in social settings.

Like a Shithouse Rat

- Meaning: Extremely excited or full of energy.
- Cultural Context: Rats are recognized for their erratic movements, which makes this expression a funny way to describe someone who is very hyper or enthusiastic.

- Example Usage: "As soon as she found out about the concert tickets, she was darting around like a shithouse rat!"
- Tips for Use: Playfully use this phrase to depict someone who is overflowing with energy or excitement.

More Birthdays Than a Cake Shop

- Meaning: Refers to someone who is quite elderly.
- Cultural Context: A bakery is filled with numerous cakes (and consequently, birthdays), so likening someone to one suggests they have experienced many years. It's a playful way to address age.
- Example Usage: "He might have more birthdays than a cake shop, but he still has the vitality of a young adult!"
- Tips for Use: Be considerate of the situation; use this expression in a warm manner rather than in a derogatory way when talking about older individuals.

More Holes Than a Swiss Cheese

- Meaning: Filled with imperfections or issues.
- Cultural Context: Swiss cheese is well-known for its holes, making it an ideal metaphor for something full of problems. This expression embodies Australian practicality and humor.
- Example Usage: "That proposal has more holes than a Swiss cheese; we should reconsider it."
- Tips for Use: Ideal for providing feedback on plans or ideas in a lighthearted yet constructive way.

Pissing Down Sideways

- Meaning: Refers to heavy rainfall.
- Cultural Significance: Emphasizes the severity of the rain by implying it's coming down at an angle because of the wind. Australians frequently use vivid language to depict the weather.
- Example Usage: "Don't forget your umbrella, it's pissing down sideways outside!"
- Tips for Use: Great for alerting others about poor weather while injecting some humor.

Straight as a Dog's Back Leg

- Meaning: Completely not straight; deceitful or untrustworthy.
- Cultural Context: Since a dog's back legs are not perfectly straight, this expression serves as a witty contradiction to illustrate dishonesty or lack of reliability.
- Example Usage: "His story's about as straight as a dog's hind leg, I wouldn't believe a word of it!"
- Tips for Use: Employ this phrase in a lighthearted manner to challenge someone's truthfulness, but steer clear of sounding too harsh.

Stands Out Like a Sore Thumb

- Meaning: Easily seen or recognized.
- Cultural Context: A sore thumb is difficult to overlook, similar to a person or object that awkwardly draws attention. This expression highlights differences or prominence.
- Example Usage: "Wearing his bright pink shirt, he stands out like a sore thumb in this group!"
- Tips for Use: Ideal for highlighting contrasts in looks, actions, or circumstances without sounding overly harsh.

That's as Helpful as a Chocolate Teapot

- Meaning: Refers to something that is entirely ineffective.
- Cultural Context: A chocolate teapot would melt before it could be used, representing the epitome of uselessness. This expression highlights the inventive humor found in Australian culture.
- Example Usage: "Getting a tent for the beach? That's as helpful as a chocolate teapot"

- Tips for Use: Employ this phrase to humorously reject impractical concepts or items.

Throw a Shrimp on the Barbie

- Meaning: Prepare food on the grill.
- Cultural Context: This phrase gained international recognition through tourism promotions, even though Australians typically use the word "prawn" rather than "shrimp." It emphasizes the importance of barbecues in Australian culture.
- Example Usage: "Let's throw a shrimp on the barbie for dinner tonight!"
- Tips for Use: Although it's not technically accurate (since "prawn" is the proper term), this expression is effective for global audiences who recognize it.

You'll Have to Wait Until the Cows Come Home

- Meaning: A lengthy period.
- Cultural Significance: Cows take a long time to come back home, making this expression an exaggeration of how long one might have to wait. It reflects a typical Australian attitude towards patience or the lack of it.
- Example Usage: "If you believe I'll stand in that line, you'll have to wait until the cows come home!"
- Tips for Use: Employ this phrase in a lighthearted manner to convey impatience or skepticism.

You Couldn't Run a Chook Raffle

- Meaning: You are disorganized or unable to handle even the most straightforward task.
- Cultural Context: Setting up a chicken raffle (a small fundraising event) is typically simple, but this expression implies that the individual is so inept that they would struggle with it. It serves as a lighthearted jab at someone's incompetence.
- Example Usage: "If you couldn't run a chook raffle, how do you plan to oversee this project?"
- Tips for Use: Best suited for informal situations among friends, it works better as a joke rather than a serious critique.

A-Z Glossary
Quick Reference to All Aussie Terms

This A-Z Glossary compiles every Australian slang term covered in the book, providing simple and direct definitions for quick and easy understanding. Each entry includes a page number where you can find more detailed explanations, examples, and cultural insights if needed. Whether you're trying to recall what "arvo" means or need a refresher on "togs," this comprehensive dictionary ensures you're never stuck for words during your travels.

A

- Anzac Biscuit – Oat-and-golden-syrup cookie. (Page: 18)
- Arvo Run – A short trip or drive in the afternoon. (Page: 54)
- Arvo – Afternoon (often used when planning outdoor activities). (Page: 28)
- Aussie Salute – Waving flies away from your face. (Page: 43)

B

- Back of Bourke – Middle of nowhere (very remote). (Page: 54)
- Bail Out – To exit a vehicle quickly (often used in informal contexts). (Page: 54)
- Barbie – Short of Barbecue. (Page: 18)
- Bikkie – Biscuit/cookie. (Page: 19)
- Billabong – A stagnant pond or waterhole. (Page: 28)
- Bingle – Minor car accident. (Page: 55)
- Bitumen – Asphalt or paved road (Page: 55)
- Bloody oath! – Strong agreement (Page: 6)
- Bludger – Someone who avoids work or responsibility. (Page: 70)
- Bogey Trap – A tissue box (used humorously). (Page: 70)
- Bogged – Stuck in mud/sand. (Page: 29)
- Bonnet – The hood of a car. (Page: 55)
- Bonza – Great/excellent (Page: 6)
- Boot – The trunk of a car. (Page: 56)
- Bottler – An excellent trip. (Page: 56)
- Brekky – Breakfast. (Page: 19)
- Bring a plate – Bring food to share at a gathering (Page: 7)
- Brumby – Wild horse. (Page: 29)
- Bubble and Squeak – Fried leftover veggies. (Page: 19)
- Bush Bash – Off-road driving through rugged terrain. (Page: 56)
- Bush Tucker – Native Australian foods sourced from the wilderness. (Page: 30)
- Bush – Wilderness, forest, or rural areas. (Page: 29)
- Bushwalking – Hiking. (Page: 30)

C

- Cabbie – Taxi driver. (Page: 56)
- Camper Trailer – A portable trailer for camping and traveling. (Page: 57)
- Catch ya later – See you later. (Page: 7)
- Cheers – Thanks / Goodbye / Good health (when toasting). (Page: 7)
- Chockers – Full or packed. (Page: 57)
- Chook Raffle – A charity raffle (often at pubs). (Page: 43)
- Chook – Chicken. (Page: 20)
- Chuck a U-ie – Make a quick U-turn, often used when navigating roads in the bush. (Page: 31)
- Chunder – Vomit (often used humorously in casual conversation). (Page: 71)
- Coldie – Cold beer. (Page: 20)
- Cooee – A call to attract attention over long distances (sometimes used in navigation jokes). (Page: 57)
- Creek – Small river or stream. (Page: 31)
- Cuppa – Cup of tea/coffee. (Page: 20)

D

- Dag – Someone who is awkward but endearing. (Page: 71)
- Dead Horse – Tomato sauce/ketchup. (Page: 21)
- Dim Sim – Deep-fried dumpling. (Page: 21)
- Dinki Di – Genuine or authentic (used to describe someone or something true to Australian culture). (Page: 43)
- Dirtie – Unpaved or dirt road (Page: 58)
- Dog's Eye – Meat pie. (Page: 21)
- Driveway – Private road leading to a house or property. (Page: 58)
- Drought Breaker – Rain ending a long dry spell. (Page: 31)
- Dunny Man – A portable toilet delivery person (used jokingly). (Page: 71)
- Dunny – Outdoor toilet, often found in camping areas. (Page: 32)

E

- Excuse me/Sorry – Apology or polite interruption. (Page: 8)

F

- Fair Dinkum Fire – A proper campfire. (Page: 32)
- Fair Dinkum Road – A long, straight stretch of road (often used humorously). (Page: 59)
- Fair Dinkum – Honestly; truly (used to emphasize sincerity). (Page: 44)
- Fair go – Give someone a chance / Be fair. (Page: 8)
- Fairy Bread – Butterbread with sprinkles. (Page: 22)
- Flat Tyre – A punctured tire. (Page: 59)
- Flat White – Espresso with steamed milk. (Page: 22)
- Footpath – Sidewalk. (Page: 59)
- Footy – Australian Rules Football or Rugby. (Page: 44)
- Freeway – A highway or motorway. (Page: 60)

G

- Galah – A fool or someone acting silly (derived from the noisy bird). (Page: 72)
- Gidgee – A type of small, hardy tree native to arid regions. (Page: 32)
- Ginger Beer – Someone with red hair (used teasingly). (Page: 72)
- Give It a Go – Try it (encouragement in social settings). (Page: 45)
- Give Way – Yield. (Page: 60)
- Gnarly – Rough or challenging (often describing roads or driving conditions). (Page: 60)
- Goanna – Large monitor lizard. (Page: 32)
- Good on ya – Well done / Good job. (Page: 8)
- Grey Nomads – Retirees who travel extensively around Australia in campervans or cars. (Page: 61)
- Groggy – Feeling hungover or tired after drinking. (Page: 72)
- Gum Tree – Eucalyptus tree, iconic to Australia's landscape. (Page: 33)
- G'day – Hello / Good day. (Page: 9)

H

- Hard Yakka – Hard work. (Page: 45)
- Hire Car – Rental car. (Page: 61)
- Hook Turn – Melbourne's unique right-turn method for trams. (Page: 61)
- Hooroo – Goodbye (old-fashioned but still used). (Page: 9)
- Hostie – Flight attendant. (Page: 62)
- How ya goin'? – How are you? (Page: 9)
- How ya gonna get there? – "How will you get there?" (Page: 62)
- How're Ya Goin'? – How are you doing? (A casual greeting). (Page: 45)
- How's it garn? – How's it going? (Page: 10)
- How's the form? – How's life treating you? (Page: 10)
- How's the serenity? – A playful way to ask, "How's the peace?" (Page: 10)
- How's tricks? – How are things? (Page: 10)
- Humpy – A temporary shelter made from bark and branches, traditionally used by Aboriginal Australians. (Page: 33)

J

- Jackaroo/Jillaroo – Young people working on farms or stations, often while traveling. (Page: 62)

K

- Kangaroo Court – Informal gathering or mock trial, often referring to outdoor events. (Page: 33)
- Kick-ons – Continuing a party/night out at another location. (Page: 45)
- Knackered – Tired or exhausted (often said after a night out). (Page: 46)
- Knock Off – Finish work or stop doing something (often followed by socializing). (Page: 46)
- Knocker – Someone who criticizes others excessively. (Page: 73)

L

- Laid-Back – Relaxed and easygoing (describes the Australian social attitude). (Page: 47)
- Lamington – Sponge cake with chocolate and coconut. (Page: 22)
- Larrikin – A mischievous but likable person. (Page: 73)
- Legend – Someone admirable/helpful. (Page: 47)
- Lollies – Candy/sweets. (Page: 23)

M

- Main Drag – The main street or road in a town. (Page: 63)
- Mate – Friend or casual address. (Page: 11)
- Mate's Rates – Discounted prices for friends or acquaintances. (Page: 47)
- Milk Run – A short, routine trip. (Page: 63)
- Mizzle – Misty rain. (Page: 34)
- Motorway – A major highway or expressway. (Page: 63)
- Mozzie Magnet – Someone who attracts mosquitoes. (Page: 73)
- Mozzie – Mosquito. (Page: 34)

N

- Never-Never – Extremely remote outback. (Page: 35)
- No Dramas – No problem; don't worry about it (used in casual conversations). (Page: 47)
- No worries – You're welcome / It's fine. (Page: 11)
- Not bad, thanks – A polite response to "How are you?" (Page: 12)

O

- Oath! – I agree / Absolutely! (Page: 12)
- Old Bomb – Beat-up, unreliable car. (Page: 64)

- Outback Highway – Long-distance roads through remote areas. (Page: 64)
- Outback – Remote and sparsely populated inland regions of Australia. (Page: 35)

P

- Paperbark Tree – A tree with peeling bark, common in wetland areas. (Page: 35)
- Pardon?/Eh? – What did you say? (Repetition request.) (Page: 12)
- Parked Up – Stopped or stationed somewhere temporarily. (Page: 64)
- Parma – Chicken parmigiana. (Page: 23)
- Pavlova – Meringue dessert with fruit. (Page: 23)
- Petrol – Gasoline (fuel for vehicles). (Page: 65)

R

- Reckon – I think/believe (used in polite or friendly conversation). (Page: 13)
- Rego – Vehicle registration. (Page: 65)
- Righto – Okay; all right. (Page: 13)
- Ripper – Excellent or fantastic (used to describe great outdoor experiences). (Page: 35)
- Road Train – Extra-long truck (common in the outback). (Page: 65)
- Rockhole – A natural pool of water in rocky terrain, often found in desert regions. (Page: 36)
- Roo – Kangaroo. (Page: 36)
- Root Rat – Someone who overeats at a barbecue. (Page: 74)
- Roundabout – Traffic circle or rotary intersection. (Page: 66)

S

- Salty – Saltwater crocodile. (Page: 37)
- Sandgroper – A nickname for people from Western Australia, derived from an insect found in the region. (Page: 37)
- Sanga – Sandwich. (Page: 24)
- Schnitty – Schnitzel. (Page: 24)
- Seeya – Goodbye. (Page: 13)

- Servo – Service station/gas station. (Page: 66)
- She'll be right – It's okay; everything will work out fine. (Page: 13)
- Shout – Buy a round of drinks (e.g., "It's my shout"). (Page: 48)
- Skite – Boast or show off (often discouraged in Australian culture). (Page: 48)
- Slushy – Slippery or muddy road conditions. (Page: 66)
- Smoko – Work break (often with tea/snacks). (Page: 24)
- Snag – Sausage. (Page: 25)
- Snot Block – Vanilla slice (pastry dessert). (Page: 25)
- Sober as a Judge – Completely sober. (Page: 48)
- Southerly Buster – Cold wind from the south. (Page: 37)
- Speedo – Speedometer or someone obsessed with speed. (Page: 67)
- Spit the Dummy – Throw a tantrum or lose one's temper. (Page: 74)
- Sticky Beak – Nosy person (used humorously or lightheartedly). (Page: 75)
- Stirrer – Someone who provokes trouble for fun. (Page: 49)
- Stock Route – A designated path for moving livestock across rural areas. (Page: 37)
- Stone the crows! – Exclamation of shock or disbelief. (Page: 14)
- Straya – Australia (pronounced 'Straya). (Page: 49)
- Struth! – Expression of surprise ("Is that true?"). (Page: 14)
- Swag – Portable bedroll for camping. (Page: 38)

T

- Ta ra – Informal goodbye. (Page. 14)
- Ta – Thank you. (Page: 15)
- Taking the Piss – Teasing/mocking (good-naturedly). (Page: 50)
- Tarred Road – Paved Road. (Page: 67)
- Thongs – Flip-flops. (Page: 38)
- Tinnie – Small aluminum boat. (Page: 67)
- Togs – Swimwear (funny because it sounds old-fashioned). (Page: 75)
- Too easy – No problem / That's simple. (Page: 15)
- Top End – Northern Australia (Page: 39)
- Track – Unpaved road (outback). (Page: 68)
- True Blue – Authentically Australian. (Page: 50)

- Tucker Bag – A bag or container for carrying food during outdoor trips. (Page: 39)
- Tucker Box – A container for carrying food to social events or work. (Page: 51)
- Tucker – Food. (Page: 26)
- Tuckeroo – Goodbye. (Page: 16)
- Tuckshop – A small cafeteria or snack bar at schools or community centers (common meeting spot). (Page: 51)

U

- Ute – Utility vehicle, similar to a pickup truck. (Page: 68)

W

- Wattle – Acacia tree (Australia's floral emblem). (Page: 39)
- Whinge – Complain. (Page: 51)
- Willy-Willy – Dust devil or small tornado. (Page: 40)
- Wombat – A small, burrowing marsupial native to Australia. (Page: 40)
- Woop Woop – A generic term for remote or rural areas. (Page: 40)

Y

- Yabbo – A rough or uncouth person (often used playfully among friends). (Page: 52)
- Yabby – A freshwater crayfish, often caught for food during outdoor adventures. (Page: 40)
- Yakka – Hard work, especially associated with physical labor outdoors. (Page: 41)
- Yeah Nah – Polite refusal or hesitation. (Page: 52)
- Yobbo – A rough or uncouth person (often used playfully among friends). (Page: 76)
- You right? – Are you okay? / Do you need help? (Page: 16)

Z

- Zebra Finch – A small bird native to grasslands and open woodlands. (Page: 41)
- Zonked – Exhausted or very tired. (Page: 76)

Printed in Dunstable, United Kingdom